Spiritual Awareness

Spiritual Awareness
God, His Word, Marriage and the Nation

Larry Roop

Imagine Poetry

Copyright

Copyright © 2019 Larry Roop

All rights reserved. This book or parts thereof may not be reproduced in any form, stored in any retrieval system, or transmitted in any form by any means—electronic, mechanical, photocopy, recording, or otherwise—without prior written permission of the publisher, For permission requests, write to the publisher, at "Attention: Permissions Coordinator," at the address below.

ISBN: 978-1-7333212-1-1

Front cover image by Oprahgraphic
Book layout by Oprahgraphic

First Printing Edition 2019

Imagine Poetry
75 Reba Ave
Mansfield, Ohio 44907

www.imaginepoetry.com

Dedication Page

Foremost to God our Heavenly Father for always being there helping to keep our marriage true, dedicated, and strong, and for showing that all things are possible with Him as our guide.

Also to my dear and loving wife Amy who I love very much, always seeing the best in me when sometimes I am not always at my best. And for her dedication and strength in the Lord, helping to always make the best of our marriage with God's help.

Epigraph

"Glorious indeed is the world of God around us, but more glorious the world of God within us."

—Henry Wadsworth Longfellow

Table of Contents

Dedication Page iv
Epigraph v
Introduction viii
{Poems About God} 1
    Believe on Him 2
    God Never Changes 3
    God's Forgiveness 4
    God's Masterpiece 5
    God's Special Gift 6
    How Strong is Your Faith 7
    Lord I Need You 8
    Shall We Pray 9
    Sometimes in Life 10
    We're Here to Honor a Man 11
    You Are There 12
{God's Word} 13
    By Every Word of God 14
    Do We Have Faith 15
    God's Strength 16
    Let Your Light Shine 17
    Love Your lord Thy God 18
    Mansions in Heaven 19
    Port in the Storm 20
    Seeking the Lord 21
    The Importance of Tithes 22
    The Measure of a Man 23

Spiritual Awareness

There is Nothing Impossible 24
Treasures in Heaven 25
Which Road Will We Take 26
Whom Do We Serve 27
Wings of Eagles 28

{Marriage} **29**
First Day of Forever 30
Nothing is Ever Impossible 31
Our Wedding Day 32
The Lord's Special Blend 33
Today, tomorrow, and Forever 34
We will Have a Lifetime 35
With You Here 36

{The Nation} **37**
Blessed is the Nation 38
One Nation Under God 39
The Second Amendment 40
The White House 41
The Wrath of God and Our Nation 42
Wake up America 43
We the People 44

Future Happenings **45**
Where to Reach Me **46**

Larry Roop

Introduction

The title spiritual awareness lends to itself something that we all need to be aware of, our spiritually in terms of God; how we perceive Him and how we perceive the world around us in our everyday lives.

As Christians there is so much we are aware of, we know as we look around that God gave us such a very beautiful place to live and everyday we have so much to be thankful for. But along with that beauty we also have the ugliness of this world, through hatred, and killings. The sin of this world is becoming more terrible everyday and we need to be spiritually aware of it all.

I broke this book of poetry into 4 categories. Poems in relationship to God; Poems based off of various bible verses (His Word); Marriage, God union between a husband and a wife; and The Nation, where it is now and where it is heading. So you see many areas we as Christians need to be focused on and be made Spiritually Aware of.

It is my hope and prayer that if you not only love poetry, but love and serve God Almighty you will find these poems in this book to be of joy and understanding in our walk with Christ.

Poems of God

Larry Roop

Believe on Him

Believe on Him always for he will see you through.
Everything that you need He will provide for you.
Live your life the way, God meant it to be:
In service to His call that others can surely see.
Everything in His time, you will always attain.
Victory is at hand, when you call out his name
Every moment you serve Him You'll have peace inside

One you cannot destroy nor even to deny
Nothing is more important, than to put Him first in life.

He will always see you through the grief and the strife.
Imagine how wonderful each day will surely be,
Making our way through life, always trusting on Thee.

Spiritual Awareness

God Never Changes

In a world full of chaos,
One thing remains true:
God never changes;
He's always there for you.

No matter how depressing
Each day seems to be,
God never changes:
He's where He needs to be.

We sometimes truly forget
That we have a place to turn
When all seems hopelessly lost,
Through many trials and concerns.

So my friends remember:
That you are never alone
Because God never changes-
He's our port within the storm.

Larry Roop

God's Forgiveness

The Bible tells us Christians,
We will always sin;
While in this human form,
The cycle repeats again.

Over and over it happens
Through each longing day:
We sin against our Savior
In many different ways.

We can't really help it,-
Its just our human nature.
We want to do what's right,
But our flesh always wavers.

A constant battle lingers
To keep ourselves in check,
But often leaves us spiritually,
An emotional mental wreck.

But the power of God's
forgiveness Is much greater than
all we do You are His special child,
And He will see you through

So pray for His forgiveness
Each time you've done wrong,
For He knows your childlike heart,
And He listens all day long.

Spiritual Awareness

God's Masterpiece

It's over for the winter,
And life starts anew.
God's hand begins creating
A masterpiece or two.

He commands every flower
To rise up again
And bring forth their beauty,
Holding their fragrance within.

Trees start their circle of life;
Each leaf begins to call,
God lays out His colorful palette
Preparing for the fall.

Grass rises to grow anew,
No longer to be restrained
And birds melodies echo
In sweet music to His name.

And so it goes, with love as well:
God places within our hearts
The beauty to see, what lies ahead
In His greatest work of Art.

Larry Roop

God's Special Gift

Son, it seems like a good time to talk,
As I tuck you down in bed,
And say the things I've wanted to say,
Not knowing how, they should be said.

Son, I think you really know
How much mom and dad love you.
And that you'll always be so special,
As you grow up your whole life through.

From the first day, into this world,
We knew you were a gift of love:
A gift that needed such special care,
That came from the Lord above.

And now that you're a little older,
Many questions run through your mind.
Some daddy can answer right now,
Others come with experience and time.

For your whole life lies ahead of you,
So enjoy it all you can;
Make the most of your younger years,
For soon you will become a man.

And someday you might be having
A father and son talk, too,
And letting him know, that he is one
Of God's special gifts to you.

Spiritual Awareness

How Strong is Your Faith

This world is leaving us shattered and torn,
Fighting a war in a relentless storm.
The enemy pushes hard to gain control;
Will they ultimately win? Will you lose your soul?

Can we go on each day standing mighty and tall,
Charging onward in battle praying never to fall?
And where is thy victory does it lie just ahead?
We need to stand firm for God's words have said:

"Your Faith should not stand in the wisdom of men,
But in the power of God" you can fight till the end.
"Fear not, for I am with you; be not dismayed,
For I am your God; I will strengthen you" this day.

"Fight the good fight of faith" and always believe
God will never forsake you He will never leave.
And be grounded in truth with words from above,
Strengthened in thy spirit, steadfast in His love.

Move forward with confidence each and every day
You can rise to the challenge you face along the way.
And no matter how strong the enemy may be
Your faith in the Lord is all that you need.

Larry Roop

Lord I Need You

Lord I need you another day
Help me and guide me along my way;
Show me the path I should take;
Help me learn from my mistakes.

I need Your strength, and all your love.
Make me the man that I once was
Before I drifted and fell apart
And lost the joy within my heart.

Help me to find what I once knew
When I lived my life all for You,
And take me back to that narrow road
That holds the future to my soul.

Spiritual Awareness

Shall We Pray

Dear Heavenly Father:
We come to You in prayer,
Ask you be with the ones
Who have lost their will to care.

Some are just depressed:
This world has let them down-
No friendly face nor loving smiles
To turn their lives around.

Then there are the ones,
Whom sickness has them drained,
Wishing they could feel no more
The heartache nor the pain.

So, dear Heavenly Father,
Be with these tonight,
Who reached out in cries of help
To find the strength to fight.

Give them what they need dear Lord,
To live life in all Your glory,
That wonderful purpose to hang on to
Retelling their life's story.

Show them how special they are
And that they are truly loved,
Teaching that all things great and small
Surely come from You above.

Amen

Larry Roop

Sometimes in Life

Sometimes in life we need to reflect
Where we stand in life's respect.
Are we doing what should be done
To ensure our life is a pleasant one?

Sure, there'll be problems along our way,
Many that will cause us to go astray,
But how we deal with these life turns
Will help us to grow in all we learn.

Keeping what matters most in our life
Would save us all from heartache and strife,
And you know if you believe upon the Lord,
He'll see you through to your final reward.

So reflect where you are, in your life now,
If things are not right, change them somehow,
For its never to late to seek what is right,
To make each day forward seem more bright.

Pray for guidance and help from above,
Believe on His words that He gave us with Love,
Trust from now on that you'll do your best
To ensure a life that He will bless.

Spiritual Awareness

We're Here to Honor a Man

We're here to honor a man,
On this very special day
Whose understanding love
Is shown in many ways,

A man who truly believes
In doing what it takes
As a husband and a father,
All for the family's sake,

A man you can look up to
And never be ashamed,
One you can be proud of
To carry the family name,

A man strong and true,
Holding to values he instills
Into the hearts and minds
Of the ones he fulfills,

And he is truly special,
Seeking guidance from above,
Sharing with his family
God's greatest gift of love.

So as we honor this man
On his loving day of rest,
I want to take this moment
To say dad, you're the best.

Larry Roop

You Are There

In a world cold and lonely,
I find comfort in where You are,
Seeking out toward the heavens,
Finding the brightest star.

I have only to reach out to You
And feel You next to me.
Soft gentle breezes flow,
Across the windswept sea.

And to have You ever near,
To call out and say Your name,
To feel the warmth of Your fire,
That glows in the eternal flame.

Always You are there,
And in many forms do You appear
You open up my longing soul
To the wonders that are so near.

You make me want to hold You close
And fill my heart's desire
With all that you share with me
And all that I acquire.

And to feel that tremendous peace
That only You can give.
Forever in my heart and mind,
You will always live.

By Every Word of God

How do we live our lives today:
Taking our path, or walking God's way?
Do we believe what's written in the Holy Book
Or glance at the pages, to have a quick look?

Is your life's foundation built on ground
To survive the ages, or come crashing down?
And when it's over, with one thing to hold
Will it be God's word, or your precious gold?

By every word of God, our lives should always be
All He intended, and all we should see,
For God the Creator would never hold us back
For its His gifts He has given, to keep our lives on track

So, take a stand now: believe what is true,
Give your life meaning, change your heart anew,
Focus on what matters, not what's strange or odd,
And live your life on fire, by every word of God.

Luke 4:4 KJV

Spiritual Awareness

Do We Have Faith

How often do we reach out
And touch the vast unknown
Or walk into the dark recess
Of places far from home?

How often do we disbelieve
That all will turn out right
Because we lack the one sure thing
That helps our line of sight?

If you believe in the Lord above,
Then you know what to do:
Ground your faith in all He is,
And He will see you through.

Hold on tight, to his words-
Let not them slip away!
He will be your guiding hand
That helps you through each day.

And let us not forget my friend
What true faith surely means:
Faith is the substance of things hoped for-
the evidence of things not seen.

Hebrews 11:1

Larry Roop

God's Strength

Lift your eyes, to Heaven,
See God's strength and love,
Believe on Him to sustain you,
Trust on Him above.

Walk with Him daily,
Believe His word is true ,
Let His light magnify,
In everything you do.

For if He can place every star,
And name them one-by-one
Shine them brightly every night,
Until the morning comes;

Then He can surely hold you close,
And never leave your side,
For He has never lost a single star,
Not one has ever died.

Isaiah 40:26

Spiritual Awareness

Let Your Light Shine

Let your light shine
Before men to see,
That where your heart lies
Is who you will be.

Show before men
All that is true,
Let your good works
Reflect upon you.

As Christians, the light,
We shine before men
Will help them to see
The power in Him.

For we want to do that,
Which will surely explain,
We do the Lord's Will
To glorify His name.

Matthew 5:16

Larry Roop

Love Your lord Thy God

Love your Lord thy God,
In everything you do.
Believe on Him always,
That He will see you through.

Hold him close within your heart,
Into your very soul,
Let His love and guidance
Always take control.

And with your inner strength,
Never give up on Him.
Even more then being your Father,
He is also your best friend.

So everyday that starts anew,
Bow your head and pray.
Look to Him and love Him,
More then words could ever say.

Deuteronomy 6:5

Spiritual Awareness

Mansions in Heaven

Mansions in heaven
There will be
A place He's preparing,
For you and for me.

For His promise He give us,
To return one day
And take us with Him
To His home far away.

He wants us to know
That where He is
There too we will be,
Because we are His.

So the mansions He prepares,
Is our eternal place
Of rest in the Lord
In His heavenly estate.

John 14:1-3

Larry Roop

Port in the Storm

When troubles close around you
And you've no place to turn,
When life treats you badly
With trials and concerns,

When all seems hopeless,
And you are down and out,
Turn to the One
Who'll remove all your doubt.

For if you fear the Lord thy God,
He will lift you up;
He'll give you a safe harbor,
When life's storms become too much.

He'll shelter you and protect you
And hold you close within,
For He loves His children,
When they look up to Him.

Proverbs 14: 26

Spiritual Awareness

Seeking the Lord

We sometimes look
In all the wrong places,
Seeking the Lord
Through innocent graces.

Our minds our not set
On things above
Or God's enduring kindness,
Surrounded in His love.

But we know from God's Word,
It's what is inside
That helps us find Him,
To use as a guide,

That from the beginning
We will have a great start,
If we seek and find Him
With all of our heart.

Jeremiah 29:13

Larry Roop

The Importance of Tithes

If I give of myself,
My tithing and time,
Giving back to the Lord,
What never was mine,

To store in his house
All that is His,
Relying on faith
In all that He gives,

He'll pour out His grace,
That we shall receive,
Giving to us,
More then we need,

Keeping His promise
To those that He loves:
Bountiful blessings
That flow from above.

Malachi 3:10

Spiritual Awareness

The Measure of a Man

Do we often sit and wonder
If we do all we can,
Wondering if the life we lead
Is the measure of a man?

Do we find it hard to project,
What God has in store,
When sometimes our faith is shaken
To the very core?

What we seek is acceptance,
Feeling we've done right,
Knowing it's not important
To hang on in the fight,

But strive to do our best,
When it's hard from the start,
Being one God chose,
As a man after His own heart.

Acts 13:22

There is Nothing Impossible

We know dear Lord,
That you have created,
The heavens and earth
And all things related.

We know you spoke,
And all came to be,
Dry land called earth
And waters called seas.

You placed the stars
In the sky at night
And the moon to guide us
By its glowing light.

But much more important,
And what is so true,
There is nothing impossible,
Or too difficult for you.

Jeremiah 32:17

Spiritual Awareness

Treasures in Heaven

Things we obtain on earth
Have no lasting appeal,
For what we hold most valuable,
Another can surely steal.

It's what we do for the Lord,
That matters most of all:
Our lives we live, to those we give,
In service to His call.

In doing so we store,
Treasures no one can take,
Nothing to destroy them,
Or cause them all to break.

And the peace that we feel,
Is all we really need
For where those treasures lie,
Our heart will also be.

Matthew 6:19-21

Larry Roop

Which Road Will We Take

Which road will we take,
In all our daily lives?
The straight and narrow one,
Or the wide one to get by?

For one leads to destruction,
And many find its path,
But few find the narrow road,
The one that always lasts.

Its so easy even as Christians,
To walk the broader road,
Not even knowing you're on it,
Until you have been told.

But keeping our mind focused,
On what the Lord had said
Will keep us on the narrow road
And His blessings that lie ahead.

Matthew 7:13-14

Spiritual Awareness

Whom Do We Serve

What is most important:
This world and all its fame,
Or serving God our Father,
Proclaiming His Heavenly Name?

Do we take up our crosses
And follow Him today,
Or serve another god
Along our journey's way?

The bible says, if we save our life,
We shall surely lose it,
But losing our life for His sake,
Then will we find it.

So why does man, knowing these words,
Want to be in control
When profiting a man to gain the world,
Will lose his very soul?

Mark 8:34-36

Larry Roop

Wings of Eagles

The Lord gives strength,
When we look toward Him,
A peace and a calm
You will get from within.

You will feel the wind lifting
As you soar from above,
You will feel His strong presence,
His strength and His love.

The journey we take,
Each step of the way,
Will renew our spirit
Throughout the long day.

Holding fast our presence,
As we walk with our Lord,
His assurance He gives us
To our final reward.

Isaiah 40:31

Marriage

Larry Roop

First Day of Forever

Today's the first day of the rest of our lives;
From this moment on we'll be husband and wife.
From the moment we say "I do" to each other,
I take only you, forsaking all others.

And "to have and to hold, till death does us part"
Is the part of our love I will keep in my heart.
For the moments we spent till our wedding day
Have made life complete more than I can ever say.

You've shown me your compassion, strength, and love,
And you've taught me to believe in the Lord above.
And if that's not enough, you've taught me to live;
To make the most out of life, to share and to give.

So, here we are now; before the Lord we stand,
Exchanging wedding vows, exchanging wedding bands.
And to you my darling husband, I will forever be true.
For now and in the future, my heart belongs to you.

Spiritual Awareness

Nothing is Ever Impossible

Darling I feel so special
To have you as my wife,
Enjoying each moment together,
As we share this wonderful life.

And knowing that you'll be with me
Through the bad times and the good,
Only further strengthens my love for you,
Just like I knew it would.

For each moment in our daily lives,
Should only get better and better
Because our two hearts are joined as one
To face life's problem together.

And with that winning combination
And the Lord by our side,
Nothing is ever impossible
To make our marriage survive.

For all any couple has to do
Is take time out to pray
Asking God for his hand in guidance,
Allowing Him to show them the way.

Larry Roop

Our Wedding Day

We are here at the church,
Two people in love,
Soon standing before men
And the Lord up above.

Our lives we once knew
Will forever be changed,
Wedding vows will be said,
Wedding bands exchanged.

Pictures soon taken,
Our memories begin,
Relatives now enter,
As well as some friends.

We'll stand before the preacher,
Who will unite us together:
Two hearts joined as one,
These moments forever.

And my heart skips a beat
As you walk down that isle;
Soon I'll stand looking,
In your face with that smile.

Your hand placed in mine,
As you are given away,
My dream will come true
On this wedding day.

Spiritual Awareness

The Lord's Special Blend

Through these difficult times,
With marriages going bad,
I look back on our lives together
And feel so very glad.

For our love, darling, is holding
All that we hold true,
All that we believe in,
Together: me and you.

Our love is standing the test of time,
The test between our hearts,
But I think we always knew my love ,
Our foundation was right from the start.

For we poured the right mixture of concrete
From the Lord's special blend,
And the walls of our lives, brick by brick,
Were also built by Him.

For we knew alone, we would fail
If we did not put Him first
And daily ask His guidance
In all our earthly work.

For He is the one who always knows
Which path to take in strife,
Giving our marriage the strength it needs
To stand the test of life.

So with the Lord's special blend
Buried deep within our lives,
Our love will stand the test of time
When He is by our side.

Larry Roop

Today, Tomorrow, and Forever

Today my darling sweetheart,
We were joined as one
Our vows we took, our hearts we gave
Husband and wife we now become.

Today this special memory
Will be etched within our minds:
A memory to keep, within our hearts
To relive through the passage of time.

Tomorrow we forge a future
That will last our whole life through.
We'll build a home, a family to love-
Together: me and you.

Tomorrow will lead to brand new days,
Each one, new wonders to share.
New challenges we'll take, walking in faith,
Talking to the Lord in prayer.

And forever there will always be
One life, where two will live,
Holding strong to the values of marriage
And all that we will give.

We will Have a Lifetime

We will have a lifetime
To share our happiness together,
Our lives to live, as one we give,
To this marriage and moment forever.

And through these wonderful feelings,
I can only ask of you
To be my wife, to share my life
In all that we hold true.

For when I first held you close,
I knew right from the start:
You were meant to be for me
And we should never part.

And I will always be there
To show you my love is real,
That you can always count on me
In how I make you feel.

So darling, always remember
To love, to laugh, to live;
And in our lifetime together,
My heart to you I'll give.

Larry Roop

With You Here

As I sit and look at the snow coming down,
I feel so warm because you're around.
Your presence here, lets me know
That I forever will love you so.

For just as God made a blanket of white,
He made you too, to be my wife.
So hold me close and keep me warm,
And I'll shelter you from the coming storm.

Together we'll protect each other, love,
As God watches from up above.
And know each day will bring to us
More joy, peace, and happiness,

Giving our life so much more
Then we could ever have hoped for,
So, as long as you are by my side,
We'll take each day as it comes in stride.

Our Nation

Blessed is the Nation

Blessed is the nation
Whose God is the Lord,
Standing strong and proud
By the writings of the sword.

A faithful nation who looks up,
Seeking God every day,
Trusting in Him always,
Along its journey's way.

A God who is just and faithful,
To see their path in life,
One who loves His children,
No matter what the strife.

To choose the ones to share,
His inheritance they deserve
Because of faithful obedience,
And a willingness to serve.

Spiritual Awareness

One Nation Under God

One nation under God
The way it was meant to be-
Forefathers fighting, living and dying
So we can all be free.

And so it goes throughout time,
Some battles never end,
Enemies we make, wars we fight,
New allies we call friends.

But somewhere along the path we've taken
We lose more of ourselves every day
And nothing we do makes up our loss
As we travel along our way.

Why have we taken God out of the picture,
When this land was built on Him?
The principles He gave us to live by
Still hold their truth within.

And yet we feel we can survive
Without Him who made us strong,
But all we've done to make things right
Turns out to be so wrong.

I think it's time we look up to Thee,
And in faith, reclaim this land
That once more, could certainly prosper
By the guidance of His strong hand

Larry Roop

The Second Amendment

There are those who want to take away
Our freedom and rights we live by today-
The ones our forefathers wrote long ago
To secure this great nation strong and in control.
But for all the amendments that are so vital,
One in particular fights hard for survival.
The second amendment that gives us all
The ability to be free and freedom to stand tall.
And all rights afford to each and every man
It so gives that right to protect our great land.
For those that support it, we stand and fight
To keep and bear arms to protect this great right.
And defend it with honor, along with the rest,
For a nation to live strong and for God to bless.

Spiritual Awareness

The White House

For two hundred years a house has sat
A safe haven and home to men
Who's job it was, to lead our nation,
Keeping it strong within.

Many names through time were given,
Important people walked its halls.
Many photographs depicting its beauty
Gave way to its splendor an awe.

And through this house it's known,
Presidents of faith were there,
Mentioning God in His wisdom
Seeking His advice through prayer.

So while It's been in ravages of war,
Surviving fire and total despair,
It stands today, a beacon of hope
For those entrusted to it care.

May the White House stand tall forever.

Larry Roop

The Wrath of God and Our Nation

There's a grave attack on our nation
From outside and within
Many are our enemies,
Fueled by hatred, anger and sin.

They think they're winning a victory,
So confident and in control,
Ready and always, poised to strike
At the heart of our nation's soul.

But at the helm of righteousness,
God stands and He leads,
Putting in place a man elected
For the sake of the people's needs.

So along with true Americans
Who are willing to stand and fight,
They will bring their enemies darkness
Into God's heavenly light.

And they will be powerless to move,
Defeated by the weight
Of God's Sword of Justice
And the people's strength of Faith.

Spiritual Awareness

Wake up America

Blessed Is a nation whose God is the Lord,
Living right unto faith, standing firm by His sword.
If only more people would commit to His Word
The line of good and evil might not be so blurred.

We're still a strong nation, one that God can still bless,
But everywhere we turn, we're in such a mess.
And what we know is wrong, we try to make right,
But through the cause of it all , we still lose our sight.

We have taken such evil and justify it away,
Hoping things will get better when we face a new day.
But, sadly, we have fooled, ourselves yet again
In believing wrong is right, and turning right into sin.

Wake up America! Hold steadfast in His will!
Let Him show you the truth that He will instill
Be a force for righteousness, in all that you do
Standing firm in His Word, that is now part of you.

Larry Roop

We the People

We the people standing strong and true,
Wave old glory: the red, white, and blue.
We believe in this nation that forever lives on
Through those that fought, to keep it strong.

We hold on to our rights that were given from above
Through God's divine grace, His strength, and His love.
And through His words, that guide our decisions
Helps us focus on our ultimate clear visions.

We strive to move forward toward one goal
That no more are we divided, but stand as a whole.
Because we the people believe this great nation
Can again shine bright through God's salvation.

Future Happenings

I want to thank you for purchasing my book, I hope you really enjoyed all the spiritual poems dealing with the four sections mentioned. There will be more spiritual poems coming out in the future.

But to let you know the next book coming out in the future will be dealing with friendships and things of that nature.

For those wondering if I plan to do any hardcover editions the answer is yes. I would love to do a hardbound edition on both my romantic poems and my spiritual poems as well.

What will be special about each one of those will be the fact that new poetry will be added to each one. In addition to the poems in the paperback versions you will get to read new poems not found anywhere else. Along with that we may even include some special gifts that you can obtain just for enjoying what I and Imagine Poetry puts out.

Where to Reach Me

If you have any comments, questions, suggestions or would just like to drop me a line saying thanks. Please do not hesitate to write me at: info@imaginepoetry.com

In the future we will be having samples of my poetry that we can send out in PDF form to those interested. Send me a note to the above address and let me know you would like a sample and we will put you on the list. Please be sure to include your e-mail address as well, especially if it will be different from the one you sent the request out on.

www.ingramcontent.com/pod-product-compliance
Lightning Source LLC
Chambersburg PA
CBHW060858050426
42453CB00008B/1016